At the Edge of the Dirac Sea

At the Edge of the Dirac Sea

poems by

Nina Pick

SHANTI ARTS PUBLISHING
BRUNSWICK, MAINE

At the Edge of the Dirac Sea

Copyright © 2021 Nina Pick

All Rights Reserved
No part of this book may be used or reproduced in any manner whatsoever without written permission from the publisher except in the case of brief quotations embodied in critical articles and reviews.

Published by Shanti Arts Publishing

Interior and cover design by Shanti Arts Designs

Cover image by Martina Angela Müller and used with her permission. www.martinaangelamuller.com

Shanti Arts LLC | 193 Hillside Road
Brunswick, Maine 04011 | shantiarts.com

Printed in the United States of America

ISBN: 978-1-951651-78-7 (softcover)

Library of Congress Control Number: 2021935740

of blessed memory

It seems to be one of the fundamental features of nature that fundamental physical laws are described in terms of a mathematical theory of great beauty and power, needing quite a high standard of mathematics for one to understand it. You may wonder: Why is nature constructed along these lines? One can only answer that our present knowledge seems to show that nature is so constructed. We simply have to accept it. One could perhaps describe the situation by saying that God is a mathematician of a very high order, and He used very advanced mathematics in constructing the universe. Our feeble attempts at mathematics enable us to understand a bit of the universe, and as we proceed to develop higher and higher mathematics we can hope to understand the universe better.

—Paul Dirac, "The Evolution of the Physicist's Picture of Nature"

And I said to my heart, *there are limits*
To you, my heart;
And to the one God.
Fish are beyond me.

Other Gods
Beyond my range . . . gods beyond my God.

—D. H. Lawrence, "Fish"

Vine a Comala porque me dijeron que acá vivía mi padre.

—Juan Rulfo, *Pedro Páramo*

Contents

Acknowledgments	11
Birkot haShachar	13
At the Edge of the Dirac Sea	15
Deixis	27
Exodus	59
Naturaleza Muerta	60
Home	62
Mother	63
Law of Motion	64
Some Notes for Teaching "My Last Duchess"	66
Dream of the Childhood Bedroom	68
Elohai Neshama	70
Making Borscht at Zen Mountain Monastery	72
Self-Portrait in Cedar and Steel	73
Dark Wings	74
Wolf Moon	75
Rain Shadow	76
Exodus	78
Dear Ariadne	79
Onyx	81
x	105
Notes	109
About the Author	111

Acknowledgments

Gracious thanks is extended to the editors of the following publications in which these poems first appeared:

Some of these poems first appeared online in an earlier form as part of the Tupelo Press 30/30 Project.

[The darkest sky is not above but down] appeared in *ISLE: Interdisciplinary Studies in Literature and Environment* under the title "The Darker Sky."

[Afterwards is a bit pale] appeared in *Poetica: The Holocaust Edition* under the title "Afterwards."

An early version of "Making Borscht at Zen Mountain Monastery" was first published in *Chronogram* under the title "Prison Sangha."

"Wolf Moon" was first published in the anthology *Dark Mountain, Book Four: Post-Cautionary Tales.*

Birkot haShachar

Blessed are you, lord our god, king of the universe, who gives us the light and the darkness.

Blessed are you, lord our god, king of the universe, who gives us the thing and its shadow.

Blessed are you, lord our god, king of the universe, who gives us the flood and the drought.

Blessed are you, lord our god, king of the universe, who gives us the form and its contents.

Blessed are you, lord our god, king of the universe, who gives us the whole of the broken.

Blessed are you, lord our god, king of the universe, who gives us the star and the atom.

Blessed are you, lord our god, king of the universe, who gives us the winged and the wingless.

Blessed are you, lord our god, king of the universe, who gives us eons and minutes.

Blessed are you, lord our god, king of the universe, who gives us the black of the morning, the last of the night sky.

Blessed are you, lord our god, king of the universe, who gives us
    the complete,
        the uttermost.

At the Edge of the Dirac Sea

A tall mountain blooms like a blister in the desert. The light here is a creation of its own, each drifting strand a humming molecule of itself. The walls are curtains, are sunburned feathers. In this place I too grow closer and closer to the arc of my being. One day I will walk through it. All places will meet like a string of mirrors over a window. In each surface I will see reflected a shard of carnivorous life. I have lived in fire and I have lived in snow and in the two at odds now battling within me. I left one coast and it was on fire. I left the other and it was sinking into the sea.

These phenomena belong, indeed, to a domain [...] where an unambiguous description is impossible.

The nature of passage is to be displaced in two places at once. Here I left the body, and here every gray nodule of the soul is blown back like ashes. So I asked God, and God curled over me like a wave over a shell, and God said, Every curved bone of the spine is a rung, and every rung is a step between the heaven and the earth, and it is here in your body that you are known and loved.

The symbolical character, in this sense, of the artifices mentioned also becomes apparent [...] in that, in using the conception of matter waves, there is never any question of a complete description.

I send myself an envelope. I seal in it every part of home I love. Snow, fog, rain, the black night, silence in winter, the smell of wood rotting on the beach. Gray pines stitching through gray sky. When I open the envelope the memories slide out, heavily, like a snowdrift. I witness my return after such long absence. I place my charred heart among the roots. I bury it in mud. There it grows worm-eaten, and slowly sweetens like a fallen apple.

> *Indeed [...] the absolute value of the so-called phases of the waves never comes into consideration when interpreting the experimental results.*

And indeed the memories form a painting of a door I could open and walk through, if only I could take hold of it. I squint through fingers at some bright street corner blindingly bright, under palm trees waving their oneiric sign. A ghostly deer clacks down the avenue like a used car. Somewhere—not here—snow falls.

In fact [...] a certain amount of latitude [must] be allowed in our account of the mutual action between the object and the means of observation.

I call to you on the telephone, but really I know it is through some viscous and visceral string reaching like a tendon to tie the bones of you to mine. I dreamed up the image, thought up the sea glass, driftwood, bolts and bricks composing such a creature, the dreaming twin, who could unscroll my body to read the tight black prayer of it. So. You arrive and stand at the foot of the bed, your horsehead cocked, your forelock falling over your eyes. Your cedar scent, your perfect shiny hooves. A key on its silver chain is resting between your breasts. All matter is spirit, obviously, you smile, your penis hardening. That is to say, when I first saw you, my soul rose up through my body and left me and entered your mouth.

This implies that a subsequent measurement to a certain degree deprives the information given by a previous measurement of its significance for predicting the future course of the phenomena.

Obviously, these facts not only set a limit to the extent of the information obtainable by measurements

Where the train tracks meet they disappear into the black archway. This is home, and the vanishing point. I believe that in exile I am untraceable. Can the dead follow me to a place they never dreamed of in life? In the landscape of the inconceived, the body is incidental, so starved and narrow it finds crawlspaces in solid walls. Yet in actuality the floodlight makes hiding near impossible. The light turns inward on darkness like a sealed envelope and betrays it.

The man comes to the door wearing a red cape. He's carrying the dreams in a box. He is very polite, bowing slightly as I open the door, and we converse for a moment on the threshold. He opens his box as if displaying a selection of fine teas. It's up to me to choose the one I want. I take a small package wrapped in felt and tied with string. Thank you, I say; he nods and bows goodbye. I go inside and place the package on the kitchen table. I eye it cautiously. Remember last night's nightmare. I hope this one is better. I hope it holds the house, the key, the gray-eyed horse who leads me home.

but they also set a limit to the meaning which we may attribute to such information.

The road runs by Bear Forest. The trees curl over the porches, and the snow is just beginning to collect, white on the black asphalt. The road reaches its arms around the land, stretching from farm to farm. In the swamp the cold blossoms bloom like bright blue moons. We were here last year, before I was gone, before we were both gone, separately. You brought your dog, who ran on ahead, and I think of you in your muck boots, and I remember loving you and your feet in your muck boots in the snow. This is the place at the end of the pathway. This I return to, here, and here again. This, my amputated, excised winter.

We meet here in a new light the old truth

A fiery orange is perched in the highest branches, suspended above the smog. Above me is this changeable citrus, and below, at the bottom of the slope, the big cracked melon of the city. It shimmers with particles in motion, its many surfaces erratic. If only I could recognize the movement inherent in all things, I could plunge my hand into these cloud-like densities, a plant, a person, a wooden table, and feel their very being reorganize around me like a flock of migrating birds. It was my father who showed me this, the inmost life of life.

that in our description of nature the purpose is not to disclose the real essence of the phenomena

It was my father who told me this. We drove home from my grandmother's in the wide night sky. And in an atom, he said, in an atom is a subatomic particle. Across great distance, his love stretched toward me like a Dirac string.

but only to track down, so far as it is possible, relations between the manifold aspects of our experience.

Deixis

*There is a pain—so utter—
It swallows substance up—*

We come to it abruptly, and at last, the harsh

Square-edge of loss. Yes there

It is. The books are piled on the shelves.

The room-smell of mother and velvet.

This is where the grief mounts up and spills

Over. This is where the grief-stricken fall

Sick and tumble. The silver veins

Of the leaf are coated in frost.

On the pond the ice is parchment thin.

It is evening in the last Basilica, blind mice

In the labyrinth of lacquered banisters, vines curling on

Its burlesque façade. Where is the way out.

This, a state of grace. There is no way but in.

I set sail on grief as if on a stream. As if grief

Were a stream I could sail down to the

Sea. It lulls me to death under the empty

Moon. There are no rations left

In the galley but rats. I hunger like a dead

Language, an island of stone.

I come to you holding my grief in my hands

As an offering, no money, just this:

See it glimmering, see it glistening, see it

Open like snow.

All it takes is one

Moment before we're down

In it scattering droplets

Like wings on water

I've dug in my heels I want

To come to rest here I do but there is

No firm ground only the

Shifting floor and the quick gash of

The not-quite-solid and besides

We're scarcely there before we're lifted

Up and out again by some sudden string we're

Pulled abruptly from the sharp edges

And the endless blue below

And below dense and dripping

As a brushful of paint and lifted

Up to the world of shapes and corners

Of ravens and snowy plovers

On the blinding shore

Unwilling to face the horror and

Unwilling to flee now that we're

Facing it we run

We kick it open.

In my dream you were

Standing by the ocean and

It was beautiful like that beach

On the island we went to last fall

Right before I left

When everything was golden

But the red rocks

They were red and I took off

My clothes behind a dune and

Lay there naked and holding

A fistful of red clay squeezed it till it

Surged out between my fingers

And I miss you as if you were

A part of my body

Cut out and absent

As if you came from mine

Instead of mine from yours.

We went to get the horse

We went to a place I had never gone

I had long desired

The hills were green and golden

Though the horse was old

And had fractured her hock

And her gray mane hung uncombed

Its beauty like the beauty of the sea

Though she would pin back her ears

And clench her jaw to refuse the bit

And balloon her ribs to stretch the girth

We bought her and took her home

I stole into the stable and into her stall

I brought her my body in flakes and pellets

My life as a barrel of water

And gave it to her in an attempt to fill

Her stark withers, her distended belly

And she accepted the gift

Of my life and my flesh

And in return stepped from her own

And left it vacant before me

The horse-body stood open as

A warm hotel, its door ajar, its red pulse beating

In a central room

I stepped into its flesh, its cavernous heart

And looked down at my own hoof legs

I could crush blood

From gold

Here, of all places, I tell you, and you're
Surprised. After all we had left together
With grand intentions and I'm back
Already. Though really all along the signs were pointing
To this. The surfaces were pulling back. Bones
Were migrating toward the skin. Time
Had come in like a ghost-ship.
We were sifting through anklebone shards.
And then I met the woman who had survived
In a cellar. And I knew it before she told me
Because I had seen her in the dream
Coated in ash. In this same way I met
My grandfather's first wife. She was fifteen when
Married, and dead, I think, by twenty.
And when I speak to her in the darkness
My eyes are shut and
When I, whispering, pronounce her
It is both a *brakhah* and a sacrilege.
It places the hammer to the fracture.
It falls where it is needed.

Surely the Lord is present in this place
And I did not know it. Standing in a
Green field in the shimmering
Stalks of frost knee-deep in the
Cold river all right I could know it. But
Here—And here—Here where the pain
Is a jagged edge. Wider than countries and
Absolute. A jagged edge tearing at the center
Like a wolf tooth, a monstrous pregnancy.
Here I did not know or trust in
The largeness of God. I knew God was
Greater than all but there was still
That one thing. There was one thing
Greater than God.
Down in the cave of the body lies
Hunger, deeper than love and
Wider than the bowl made
To hold it, and true
To its nature, it consumes
Its own shore and
Flooding over, becomes
Starvation, the pool at

The body's center that

The body drowns in.

Here in this place God is no light-

Being but a wolf-mother eating

Her cubs and she gives and she

Takes away she takes away she

Takes away until there is no

God left but remainders.

If we feed it, it will just grow larger.

Its skeleton immense, its limitless and

Hollow belly. It will turn to towering pain.

Its right side empty its left full of fire

Running up a smokestack spine. I tell the men

Do not feed this creature it will become a

Monster. You will feed it with your own life.

It will eat you whole and leave the hinges

Of you strewn across the lawn. I say

Do not feed it. But the men come with their

Hands outstretched as if seducing a deer.

They offer a generous ounce of their ashen hearts.

The creature will take it gently, her soft muzzle

Tickling their palms. She will be gracious and

Thankful. She will love their love.

Later, I will pick up pieces

Of their shoes and I will sigh.

God said no but the snake said

Yesss. So who is to be blamed

If Eve ate the apple then ate the apple tree then ate the snake.

I had steered into a cul-de-sac. I was

Not-thinking of it

Everyday. What is there

I do not know about. Only the pain

Is a lucid dreamer. In the dream

I sleep when the dream requires

Running. In the dream I sleep

While the sleep shudders under me

And all there's left to do is

Run. And still sleeping

Our lips meet and when I wake

We are kissing.

Dry as the Atacama in winter and sun-stripped

To the white bone I could not get where

I was going I was

Still unbroken I was still

Fighting the pitch and the steel

I would have to turn

To trace footprints through dead sea to

Tunnel in to unbury and exhume

I could not would not was fully unwilling to

The past was heavy as salt

Or snow I was encrusted in it

One by one I had

Lopped off my frost-spurred limbs

Encased and entombed

I could not run there

Was nowhere to go

Riding the train from Grand Central Station I had tried
It yesterday for the first time and
As the buildings skated by leisurely and
Graffiti-covered I felt that first kindling of
Desire that was love and also fanatical
Desperation a desire like a Savoy knot its
Answer its question its fulfillment its cause
And I was glad and also outraged that I was stuck
On a train now passing the small towns and the
Rain-wet woods and the first greening hills because
Had I not been trapped had I not been stuck to my seat
By my one-way ticket and the fluttering pages
Of the *New York Times* and the train's rapid
Northward motion had I been able to seek
I would have sought and had I sought
I would have found and even then sailing through the now
Beautiful Berkshires as if on a raft in an otherworldly
Sea I suspected that once again would have been
Twice would have been a lifetime and a short one at that
But all the same once I had glimpsed the branches
Pushed aside had seen the leaves peeled back and

Burning and the terrible light and known the face of the

Sacred the divine enumeration that

Through the door or through the vein

No matter enters as it can

Then I was bereft

For how could I find God now

How could I find God now

So this is the traveling. We are

Here, for the time being. Not in a place

Light-marked by a square of light

On the floor. Not in a moment still

Lifting and folding like a

Wave. The tree is catching

Fragments of sky

While we struggle to do

Our slight work in the

Right way, and kind.

Which to string and which

With the gasping gills

To pity and toss back. To eat

Though it is our tongues

We eat, and the muscles of

Our mouths.

The light waves move like a

School of scattering fish

And this too is a way of being

In a place.

We are here, if we means

I and are means was

And here means

Not at all.

Buzzards circling the bay we drive

Through a light falling like knives

Until crossing into the luminous floodplain

Just when we thought we'd rather leave

And be done with it forever

We reach at last the heart of the matter

The light is alive its thousand vicious

Wings beating

Its dark belly spinning with flies

I know to run from this sharp-edged

Monster called the

Numinous

This is how God shows up when we're

Not looking

So easily mistaken

For something human and desired

It is by your longing

You will be destroyed, says God in

Desire, His most fearsome sign.

The waves ratchet higher.

The glass-seeds splinter. It is a windy day

This, the end of the world. The children

Playing in their flooded pens.

When I speak you say nothing.

When I speak you say nothing at all.

When finally you speak you unleash

A huge wave of silence

Like spilling honey. It is

To lead us through the maze

Of the sublime.

Here at the apocalypse

Everything is growing

Smaller and softer.

I pick from the bin a

Crushed avocado

Its green flesh rotting

Under broken skin. Oh dream, it is

Clearly my heart.

Don't press too hard, you say

Just hold it lightly.

Well, too late now.

It is made of flesh. It is

Already bruised by the sun.

The code is a tunnel stretching from

One realm to another and when you whisper it

You are granted entry you are

Welcomed back to that place which is

Always there contiguous

And this time you may arrive

At a different field a different rock

But nonetheless you recognize it as

A form of home you wish

You'd lived in more and longer

Here where you meet the deer's bright eyes

And the long gaze of the day

And one time you invited me and I

Went with you

We lay side by side our fingers intertwined our

Hips touching and as if in a dream of flying

I went there too

Except before me the tunnel opened into a black hole

And in the nothing I saw

Nothing and then

The helix

ragged tearing rotting

What I had forgotten

It had never forgotten

What I had longed for

It had never longed for

Its twin vines were dancing

Equidistant from each other

Skating endlessly around an

Impenetrable absence

Like star-crossed lovers

Held in place by the

Distance between them

The darkest sky is not above but down

At the roots, down

Where the heart is pummeling

And pounding pounding its fists.

Beneath boredom and apathy and sheer banal

Annoyance is the stark outcry

Why, and anger, that it should be

So. In the end, though, given a choice

Between being and not-being

I'd rather be. After all, I like it here.

Even when I thought I'd rather choose

Burning or drowning

Than life, as if I had a choice, as if the

Living were other than

The burned and the drowned.

Leaving the forest, my heart will

Flame up in its sage- gray

Fur. I will go trailing behind me forest

And forest and forest. Thank you, world

For having had me. You're a delightful host

Though I, at times, am the most ungracious

Of guests.

I fear I'm breaking holding

It in my arms the body on splints

In its shattered dome. Holding it

As a great scroll, strung to nothing

But the small and obdurate bones.

Yet the dream says, faith.

You are surrounded by love.

When at last it is time

You will know it

When called to prayer

You will go.

I reach my hands into it
Up to the elbows I was
Led here when I thought
We were heading some-
Place else I had thought
It would be gone by now
But it's not no not at all
It's still the box in which
We hide from dreaming
What it was, and what
It's come to now. These
Quiet dreamless beasts
Are hard to follow home
Wings turn like leaves
On glass-eyed branches
The mouse lies dead in
The driveway where the
Tabby killed it no one has
Tidied up no one has
Kicked it gone. It's been
Eaten out by maggots its

Stomach churning its

Heart licked clean. When

I think of love I think of

This. Revelation, arrived

At last. From revulsion

You are indiscernible.

I couldn't look and then I looked.

The petals curled around snow as if around a cool

Fist. Suddenly came suddenly and then

Departed. At the center a many-limbed sorrow was

Spidering outward. Some dark fleck

Of being fought hard against the yolk.

All the animals had lined up

To wait by the wall. They will be there

When I call for them I know

I just have to call. Come horse come bull come

Otter come crow they come with nightfall

Held in tooth and paw. Hey you I am ready I am

Ready now come.

Afterwards is a bit pale

Like the morning after a trip

When the lights return to stasis

And every bright hologram is

Now one dull point and you

Recall just barely that some

Dark portal had opened above the abandoned

Station and you had walked on through

As if it were a rip in a velvet curtain

And upon enfolding yourself

In the mangled fabric discovered

You would never return

So it is after the loss the slow emergence

From the dream and the nothing

Into the where

Where something is broken

The gradual remembrance of a

Wild grief, a raging, a refusal

Opening into the canyon where

No refusal is possible, and then

What is gone, still gone.

Exodus

Then covers the Abyss with Trance—
So Memory can step

Naturaleza Muerta

Whether for tradition's sake or
Superstition, I do not know,
But I learned, perhaps from
My father's father, who
Was a tailor, or from
My mother's mother,
Who sold clothing at
The family store,
Never to darn the shirt on a living
Body, and if you must,
You should give the body something
To eat while you do it, as a symbol
Of life.
What horrors would occur, if
In a rush out the door, we stopped
To fix a seam, and meaning to repair,
Knit the body in,
The buttonholes
Of the flesh stitched shut like
An *invunche*,
And mended at last.
What error, if
Patching the vessel, we
Built a cocoon.
Is this how we shroud our dead,

In skirts and blouses, dressed for the party,
Or is this the still life of the living:
My mother on her knees,
My mouth full of thread;
Wooden bowl, apricots, flies.

Home

In trying to reclaim feelings specific to
                                      the past
It's best to remember not the place time or
                                      history
But only the lay of the lake and how the
                                      constellations
Scattered
From where you looked as you were falling
                                      back
In the dark water
In the end you don't remember his or her
                                      name
Or the room where you worked or the words for
                                      things
But only how the sweep of the field was
                                      different
Depending on the morning's weather and how the
Road curved up and lifted its wings at the horizon
And how you walked it strung full with disbelief and
Gratitude and how you swore you'd never leave it
                                      and you did

Mother

the eggs
are shocked in
the ice water then
stripped from their
shells I'm similarly
dismantled by the
sudden glaciers
in her love

Law of Motion

It seemed the light was streaming in
Through the window like a summer afternoon
Or a rosy dawn or the blushing fingers of God
And so lovely that for a second I didn't
Wonder what it could be or mean but only lay there
Staring as ruddy ballerinas danced over the ceiling and
Down the walls like I was alive
And in a kaleidoscope or floating
In a tidepool belly-up and
Dead at last
And it wasn't until I saw the clock and heard
The sudden unfamiliar crunch of steel on snow
That I understood that it was four a.m.
And everything I believed in
Was, in fact, wrong.
I rose stumbling from his warm body and threw on his hoodie
Which went down to my knees
And thus clothed and stinking
Of stale smoke and Old Spice
I ran outside
To find the car high in the bed of a tow truck
Bundled in chains.
And as the car was raised higher and
Higher and therefore progressively
More difficult to retrieve, I became

In equal magnitude and opposite direction
Less and less high until
Abruptly sober, my bare legs
Burning, I stood in the drift in the night
In a truth stark as air:
I couldn't figure out I simply did not know
How I had gotten from there to here
With some guy from high school my
Car parked on his curb in the way of the plow
Gotten home from the bar and
So many miles away from
My life.

Some Notes for Teaching "My Last Duchess"

The trenchant word being
Last, as in, "The last pain that
She makes me suffer" (cf. Neruda)
Or "The faded blue / Of the
Last remaining aster flower" (cf. Frost),
Signifying late and final, lost and
Absolute, falling somewhere between
A duchess, nevermore, and one who's
Just not around, and if in conversation
The *last* is emphasized, it may suggest
The duchess most recent and freshest
In memory, i.e. the one before you,
My dear and present Duchess,
He might say over dinner,
The thought accompanied by a lingering
Twinge, a brief sigh of regret.
See at the end how the duke
Brags about the seahorse
Statue, and wouldn't you, if you
Had a bronze Neptune
In your dorm room, rather than
Talk through some dour memory
Of your dead wife.
The point being, of course,
Just when you think you've resigned the

Last of the duchess, consigned her corsets,
Placed her jewelry in storage, sold her folios
At Blake's Discount Textbooks, the
Darling ghost, the darkling
Thing appears, just like my ex,
Who texts me
Whenever, for a moment, I forget!

Dream of the Childhood Bedroom

Here
I found you
Or you found me

I pull you on as
My sleek crow suit
The one

With the hood and the beak
And the hanging threads

Dressed in your cape
In your overlarge
Shoes I can tell

You want for once
To hunger
As animals hunger

Without shame

With just the
Sharpened edge of
A hunter's fever

I slip into your
Voluminous sleeves
As if you stood

Behind me and I stood
Swaying
In your arms

To the silence
Of the recurring dream

In your hunger
Such as it is

All my blossoms blushing
In your low-moon mouth

Elohai Neshama

> *Then the angels saw / how He divided them:*
> *the man, the woman, and the woman's body.*
> —Louise Glück, "Lamentations"

We sit
Legs bent two halves

Of a lotus a
Broken shell a smashed
Melon

Wings sealed under skin
Ungrown

I had abandoned one part where the coast was in flames
Another where the sand was sinking into the sea

One part came with me
To the stranger's bed

Still burning

That is to say not one
Not even one

To tell the truth

I had as I entered cut
Soul from flesh

Shaken it off and left it
Where it lay

Some foreign
Thing

In the doorframe

Splay of feathers
Wreath of kelp

Faithful unwanted dog who loved me

And whom I wanted to love
But would not sully my hand to touch

Making Borscht at Zen Mountain Monastery

The paring knife slips under the skin,
Eases under black-purple wrinkles, loosens
The dry casing. It slices through lush musculature,
Through minuscule juice-bearing veins.

The knife runs around the scalp, removing the final
Brittle tuft of hair, then descends
To the belly. It amputates the shriveled umbilical,
The last lick of the mother tongue.

In beets up to our elbows, we are talking about
Death row. I say, Kogen once told me
That when convicted for murder, he spent
Eight months in solitude counting his breath.

The irony is not lost on me: I too am here
To learn about impermanence.
Before the meal, I bow at the altar. My clasped hands,
Stained with juice, rise like a low red moon.

Self-Portrait in Cedar and Steel

The blue veins on the back
Of her hands are like a faded draft of
Desire penciled in on graph paper
You've seen it before but who remembers
Who cares to remember how or
When after all you came crawling in
Your palms stuccoed with blood
To the one place you could still find
Shelter and it was such a map
That led you there it was
In Nietzsche's words both the abyss
And the rope across
And as it's too soon
For mercy and too late
For amends you make
Sculptures of your excised
Pieces a life-sized lion
Towering in your sister's kitchen
A three-legged horse
On the front lawn
One leg each for the
Women you slept with
And one leg missing,
For your wife.

Dark Wings

The crow in fascination
Eats his shadow and becomes it.
So do I, and so do I become.
My claw at your claw, my beak
At your beak. I do know
That to eat is a form of loving.
My grandmother served
Gray lumps of meat, pallid
Cauliflower steeped
In vitriol like a brine,
White bread, despair.
And though the chicken
Might be poison, and
Though she had pulled
The margarine, veined
With mold, out from
Under the sofa cushions,
I would eat willingly
Every bite, so as not to
Waste a crumb of
All that fury.

Wolf Moon

We shoe the horses
And the dogs, while we're at it.
And why not? I've grown
So ill-accustomed to nature
That when I woke, in full light,
I thought it was the glow of morning
Or the LED lamp in the hall.
All my figures
Are phantoms, flattened like roadkill
And covered in flies. When's the last time
I saw a living creature for a
Sharp-nosed comparison?
We were the sly-as-foxes,
The gentle-as-doves, the
Lion-hearted, the eagle-eyed;
Now we languish, unmoored
In the swamp of language,
Heartless and blind.

(Your sorrow is your lifeline, Wolf replies. Hold on.)

Rain Shadow

Though lacking antler, fang
Or pluck I can make it happen
I can take nail to rind when desperate
For something sweet when anything
Broken and spitting will do
Like a fire hydrant on a hot day
We can run through
Its spray of prisms
All morning long
All night.
So the crash
And shatter was an accident
You think, you think
I didn't want to
Break it open I didn't
Want to fuck shit up?
That was the point of it, after all
I followed him in
After all I've had enough
Of the solitary voyage the
Long journey to the sun.
I take off my feathers
Their edges coated in wax
And I lay down my crested
Helmet and my leather flats

And down to the flightless skin
Surrender
Shell and piston
Rudder and oar.
I'm ready at last for you,
World. I'm
Ready at last
For you.

Exodus

As the story goes
Each of us has a flaw
Inborn and absolute
As Pharaoh had his
Hardened heart and
Our life's work is
To mend the rent
At the very spot where
The stitches catch.
My heart not
Hardened but marsh-like
Soft is alert to its own
Quandary
The thread pulls rain
Through air
Dear god please
Repair
I want
To be a glass
For water
I want
To love in service
Of love.

Dear Ariadne

Though it seems
As if it were taking me
Into the labyrinth
Guiding me through dark
Passageways around corners to the
Pool at the center with
The minotaur standing on the
Edge glowing red and
Surrounded by bones
Though it seems it propels me
Forward at the same time
As it goes unraveling
Behind me, ultimately
It doesn't lead to death. It is
The rope I can tug from the
Bottom of the well
To let you know I have
Changed my mind.

Onyx

*Around—across—upon it—
As one within a Swoon—*

She goes down because she can.

For no other reason does she make the descent.

It would seem there is a choice involved.

This is a key point.

No victim, but victor, she lays upon the earth
                                  with the lathe of her body.

Her love is a form of curiosity.

What starts as curiosity ends as possession.

A woman doesn't speak of such things often.

A leaf fallen on water, ebb, spiral, eddy.

Weightless, she has no way, no words, to say it.

To say, I loved you so much I took you with what I carried.

With only the tools I was made with.

Here is one way I have known love:

As a vacant room, floor slick with blood, tide rising.

The air, wide eyed, sinking down to meet it.

And four walls, which bend and shatter.

We stand, hands clasped, at the threshold of a burning house.

This is one of the ways I have known love.

To say it is luminous is to make it so.

In a great space something unfolding.

I join hands in a gathering of trees.

When we step at last from the circle I sense, though unknown, the delicate opening.

As a fist holding an offering, a skein of sensation as light.

You accept this gift, in the small ways you know how.

Down on the grass, blades of evening cutting through dying petals.

My heart, wet on its bone branch, shivers.

I lie with my head toward the mountains where the train comes.

It enters my brain like a spine.

My feet towards heaven.

Our bodies are carvings on the rocks.

They are holding hands.

It was in this form that I was conceived.

And it was in this form that my mother brought me into the world.

There she lies on the ancient stonework, dreaming me.

Like a centaur, part human, like a pegasus, part crow,
                              you are on your way to be born.

You eat from the deep green grass of your mother's womb.

Your still-soft hooves grapple with rocks.

Your fur is downy and sheer with sweat.

Come into the world, and meet me, creature of dream.

This is my invocation.

Trembling, you hang from the womb like a bat,
                                      encircled in wings.

I find you at last in the leaves where you fell,
                                where you gleam like an onyx.

You speak, your first words. Your new-formed language.

We exist, you say, *because of our edges.*

I love that, I say. I write it down.

The ley lines cross and I'm sprawled at their center.

Though the dream doesn't say it, I can read between the lines:

I'm coming feetfirst into the world, black cord around neck.

And when you cry, I laugh; it's the emblem of ambivalence.

The ancestors swing their kites in an open field.

Each wing is made of memoir and jawbones.

Each string a hanging wire.

Finally the words return to the ink that made them,
                                                    and pour down.

Their sludge streams over me like acid rain.

I want to learn instead the soft cord of the heart.

The part that leads me to you and your eager, bright-faced pain.

Yet when you turned towards me I turned away.

You came to me with your skinned knees bloody and I laughed.

The body clenches around an absence.

A vacuum in the shape of whatever fits inside it.

A fiction so real the body responds in turn, with truth.

The flesh comes forth with a gift, a gesture, willingness.

Then rage, a fury like a smashed rose.

Twice I come shuddering to this threshold.

First for shore, and then for water.

First for man, his body as a plane, a kind of mowing, and then for woman.

Her thighs, her fingers of brine.

For night, then shadow.

Cold on the bleak rock, the water crashes down around me.

This is where I go when I come.

I dedicate the merits of this practice to:

Rabat Atirat Yammi, who walks on the sea.

Because you were kin, I came.

Brother, lover, mirror, I held you to me.

I laid my head down, nonetheless, in a stranger's palms.

I said, let me love like this.

If I could love like you I could love:

As two hands clasped to the ax.

This tangle of breakable bones, cracked skin,
                            can strike a match, break glass.

Underneath, the sap runs sweet.

World, where should I turn?

Here, always here.

Even water burns.

Sea-smoke rising from a driftwood house.

May I be a hollow for your love.

As a shell lying open on the shore.

The innerskin iridescent, the surface wet.

I spelled, my love, your name out on the sand.

The address of a formal letter.

In times of desperation I'll come to this.

To prayer, and to petition.

It could be read from both above and below,
                             as if etched on glass.

I didn't know if you resided in the sea-gray sky.

Or underground in the shale and the flesh.

Or if you were the sand itself and I wrote to you
                          in your own many points of being.

Or if you knew already, with no need for writing.

Here I come to the limits of our letterpress language:

I want to raise storms, ghosts, armies, not thoughts, not words.

I took off my clothes, thinking nudity a form of worship.

A way of being naked before you.

I would strip off the excess, as one strips fat from the meat.

I would appear before you as if pure from the mikvah.

I would emerge from the water as a strong, clean bulb,
                                      solid and cool to the core.

Under the rainfall of your love I would shoot stems
                                      edged like a knife.

When and if I loved, I would love clear to the hilt.

What a trial to drag around the body, as a heavy shirt
                              drooping from the bones.

Each day, shocked and jolted, unfolded from its strata of dreams.

From layers of tissue translucent as feathers, shook.

In moments like this I hate life.

Or at least the ways it makes itself known.

As ceaseless action.

Throughout the morning, tendrils curl
                    sleeping in the warm pockets of the body.

You move slowly, legs apart, arms held from sides,
                              to avoid igniting.

Yet inevitably you turn your head and there it is,
                              the wreck, the accident.

Skin greets skin and the point of impact
           is like the scent of the lemon tree.

Its year-round fruit.

Every love has heartbreak buried within it.

Either there is no great love, and it ends.

Or there is a great love, and it ends later.

Or there is a great love, and it ends after a lifetime of loving, in death.

Or there is a great love, and it never ends but breaks, like water.

There is no self, wrote Goffman, just masks, all the way down.

You come off crumbling in my hands.

A chalkdust stain on my clothes, your carcass bones.

Wrist-deep in your disintegrating center, I open my fist.

As the scene erupts, we escape,
                             carrying everything, nothing, we need.

Your body, my body, and the dead dog, still crucial,
                             laid out on the floor.

I watch the lights sliding over the windshield and down
                             the body of the truck.

A notion of peace, though we lie in a black pool of blood.

One way, I suppose, of coming clean.

I slip into the past as if slipping into a glove.

The wolf-bird, the raven, flies along the horizon.

Its silhouette is a portent, it rolls in like clouds.

It carries a thin gold band of retrospective knowledge.

This is the loss doubled over.

What foresight would have saved, if it could save.

What hindsight salvages, compulsively, if it could salvage.

Faith comes in like a bride in a haze of chiffon.

We stand at last under one moon, this mercifully secular god.

The black horses arrive at nightfall.

The herd comes as one, then spills like glass.

An endless eye, its bottomless pool.

The overturned bowl of a hoof. A fluted ear.

Under a raging sky, under a furious black-hooved sea:

I raise the wine of my own crushed body, in thanks.

The room is hung in gradations of shadow.

A chevron of smoke glides past,
               made of a thousand transparent wings.

The eye of each wing flicks open, open, open, then shuts.

Your ghost lives here as silver cased in velvet.

Your ghost lives here in its vetiver gown.

In its billowing shroud, as if you stepped forth from the fog.

And kneeling on the deck, you reached out your hand
                             to save me from drowning.

And I was drowning, not in water but in air.

I remember your nails, they were yellow rimmed and cracked
                             like teeth.

And your hands, clamped at my throat, as a necklace of bone.

In the darkness, a lace curtain lifts at the open window.

Night turns like a lock.

What pleasure, finally, to travel and leave the body behind.

A suitcase packed tight and abandoned on the train.

To leave all the fantastic catastrophes of the body.

Its pinched nerves and desperate quantities.

Its how many inches of flesh to the bone.

I come to you, and your long lean arms.

We meet, in the shadow of the station,
                in our herringbone suits, like wolves.

In the darkness now your skin is wet with sweat.

In the darkness now you stand behind me.

As if my body were the masthead of a ship, and you, in wings and sails, the ship.

Its weighted hull sunk deep and flecked with spume.

My hands are crossed at my wooden keel.

This is one of several ways I have known love.

A wind blows through a dark room.

The drains are clogged with leaves.

When the rain comes, it will stream down from the roof.

Sleek hair parting over skinny shoulders.

Overnight every vine on the lattice will bloom.

Each with its clenched fists, its tiny spiraling curls.

We will wake to the still-deepening dream of the morning glories:

Foxglove, hyacinth, the early blossoming peas.

We will stand, as the black horse in the pasture stands,
                                        awash, for once, in light.

In the distance, the bells are ringing in the clock tower.

In the distance, the freeways spin, and spinning, sing like snakes.

How could I be here, and hating it, find a way to love.

The earth, gagged in pavement, sutured with pipelines.

As loving the child with the dirty face requires

a learning to veil, or not to feel, a wave of distaste.

It is time to rise for the Amidah, and still no words come.

No words, but finally, blood, and the burning edge of song.

Adonai, s'fatai tiftach ufi yagid t'hilatecha.

Mute, I pray only to love the form.

Praise God for the wetness in things.

The viscous juice in an aloe.

The blue pool in a trout.

Its puddled self, its reckless spill of roe.

The old, damp sheets of fog dripping in the rain.

Your hummingbird mouth in the trumpet flower.

Its dark red notes.

And the wet in the floodlet body, its ebb and swell
                                      a form of making space.

Of loving more, and better.

And in an apple, its luscious honeycomb cells.

The flood and the glut.

The barren rock.

The mansion of language.

An empty room.

Many with wings.

One sharp thing.

So which would you choose, if you could choose?

The prison of flesh or the prison of bones?

The streets are lined with funeral pyres, the shops nailed shut.

Love holds you to the catastrophe.

One hand is cupped around the soft red fruit.

One hand is cupped in the space within.

The fist unfurls its petals of nails.

When the night terrors begin, we dream the same dream.

We are crawling through a thousand empty rooms.

The rooms are empty so that there is room for grace.

We enter the rooms, one by one, until grace comes.

x

*Goes safely—where an open eye—
Would drop Him—Bone by Bone.*

When the end comes it comes like sunk iron.

It plunges overboard and sinks into the past

as if into the flesh of an enormous fish.

The flesh collapses like a ruined city.

The stonework stands but the rivers burn.

Standing at the helm I grasp

a flaming wheel of petals. We sail through

its jagged eye.

Our flesh holds us to living,

holds us to dying,

holds us to the words nailed by the door of our life.

How awesome is this place,

I did not know it.

The beauty meets the horror how the sea meets the sky:

in blinding light.

For the ancestors

Notes

Epigraphs:

Dirac, P. A. M. "The Evolution of the Physicist's Picture of Nature." May 1963. *Scientific American.* 25 June 2010. Web. 14 March 2013.

Lawrence, D. H. "Fish." *The Complete Poems of D. H. Lawrence.* London: Wordsworth Editions, 1994.

Rulfo, Juan. *Pedro Páramo.* Mexico: Editorial RM & Fundación Juan Rulfo, 1955.

Dickinson, Emily. Poem 599. Ed. Thomas H. Johnson. *The Complete Poems of Emily Dickinson.* New York: Little, Brown and Company, 1960.

Dirac Sea:

Italicized sections are excerpted from Neils Bohr. Ed. J. Klakar. *Foundations of Quantum Physics I.* New York: Elsevier Science Publishing, 1985.

Deixis:

"[Dry as the Atacama in winter]" is inspired by the film *Nostalgia de la luz.* Dir. Patricio Guzmán. Atacama Productions, 2010.

Exodus:

"Notes for Teaching 'My Last Duchess'": This poem is after

"My Last Duchess" by Robert Browning. *In Poetry: An Introduction and Anthology.* Ed. Edward Proffitt. Boston: Houghton Mifflin, 1981.

The Robert Frost quote is from "A Late Walk." *The Poetry of Robert Frost: The Collected Poems, Complete and Unabridged.* Ed. Edward Connery Lathen. New York: Henry Holt and Company, 1975.

The Pablo Neruda quote is from *Twenty Love Poems and a Song of Despair.* Trans. W. S. Merwin. New York: Penguin Books, 1969.

"Self-Portrait in Cedar and Steel": Nietzsche, as paraphrased by James Hollis. *Swamplands of the Soul: New Life in Dismal Places.* Toronto: Inner City Books, 1996.

"Elohai Neshama": Louise Glück. "Lamentations." *Descending Figure.* New York: Ecco, 1981.

Onyx:

Goffman, Ernest. Cited in *The Blank Slate: The Modern Denial of Human Nature.* Steven Pinker. New York: Penguin, 2002.

x:

"How awesome is this place" quotes Genesis 28:17.

I would like to express deep gratitude to everyone for their help with bringing this book into form: Rabbi Jill Hammer; Elsa Khalfin; Ellery Akers; Christine Cote of Shanti Arts; Paula Baver; Jessica Headley; and my parents, Sheila and Peter.

Nina Pick is the author of two chapbooks, *À Luz* and *Leaving the Lecture on Dance*, and editor of *The Gardener Says*. Her poems have appeared nationally and internationally in numerous journals and anthologies. A resident of Massachusetts, she is an oral historian with the Yiddish Book Center and has a private practice in Integrative Spiritual Counseling, focusing on dreamwork, embodiment, and intergenerational healing. ninapick.com

SHANTI ARTS

NATURE · ART · SPIRIT

Please visit us online
to browse our entire book catalog,
including poetry collections and fiction,
books on travel, nature, healing, art,
photography, and more.

Also take a look at our highly
regarded art and literary journal,
Still Point Arts Quarterly, which
may be downloaded for free.

www.shantiarts.com

www.ingramcontent.com/pod-product-compliance
Lightning Source LLC
Chambersburg PA
CBHW022107040426
42451CB00007B/160